Grazing the Wallp _ ... ...a..ty.

Theory in mystic experience.

Table of content:

Grazing Reality glass
Projections on the wall
Entry once
Template poem no 1.
Electric stroller on the mozzarella engine.
Diamond rotation in Silicone Valley
Injection projection
Squeeze brain between fingers
Rainbow blade sledge
***

Teoria Realia:
Confessions on the stake.
Swim!
She who has become counscious of Truth

Extras.

Grazing the Wallpaper of Reality.

I'm in a box filled with cotton wool pool
surrounding my body

in weightless primordial soup of
Nothingness.

Swim in a cotton pool.

 Weightless body rest on the cotton candy
floss cloud,

I swim in glassy wool smooth wrap around
the head

like turban warming up brain electric
system of plugs USB ports

where I sail like drunken ship lost between
words on the Ocean of Nothingness.

Blinded by the light leaking out of cosmic
womb

square one of all squares in navel of
goddess astronomical stomach stretched
on the wheel of fortune growing like a tree
of life in my living room by the window.

I roll a joint with grass to send me mellow
mood

in haze over my brain.

Swimmer in a river of words coming out on
a keyboard of my computer.

Tips of my fingerprints leave traces on a
glassy liquid

screening of my thoughs in spiral spin into
centre of everything dimmed blackness.

Tip of iceberg floating around like shelf

fully frozen goods stacking the shop with
sweets on a windowsill.

Not one poster which we printed there
going to fill up walls of Bearpit.

I am in a mood for climbing highest
mountains in the world. On the path to the
top I march together with other sherpas
ready to give life to get there.

On the top we can smoke and get high on
the top of the world.

Grazing the wallpaper of Reality

Printed in geometric patterns floating in a
field of vision

looks like British flower designed old
school walls

floating patterns break dimensions
conntinuuity

perception allow to lift flaking off wallpaper
sheets

dismantled multilayered construction
matrices embedding printed

patterning in numerology equations of
single number powers

vibrating in space

I bite on the corner block builders

construction of holographic film projection of

my mind.

I see thin layer filming time-space capsule of the subconscious.

Diving in a waterfalls falling off rocky shelf

streaming foam of story to be told

so I write down what comes my mind

download from the source data packets, coded messages.

I unpack them zip.com

converting myself into cosmic antennae

lighted up like beacon of pirate radio station.

Saved electronic plug ins USB port

call my drunken ship from rocky waters on

the Ocean of Nothingness

swims on waves lost in a misty sea.

Lantern sends Snapshot of lights to lead
my drunken ship

across the endless waters to the USB port
plug in on memory stick with my poems.

Grazing wallpaper on the glassy walls of
Reality

which layers flake off in layers sticking out
rolling edges

where plaster crushed out.

Firstly wallpaper protect inside flesh fillers
in alive, mass psychosis deformed
impression on machinery system Reality
structure.

Mental construction made of Lego blocks

spreading in square building odd flashing
in colours projection

on crystalline screen of retro computer
C64.

My eye is CCTV camera for the researching
depths

of realistic structure.

I bite again chewing electrons rotating
around my tongue

in empty building block taste is sour like
old milk,

I puke out all content which converts into
series of patterns coded numerology of
reinveted archaic language.

Mathematic equation for golden ratio.

In letter Pi I find reason to search
sunflower sutra session consuming
bombastic sun beam of healthy fats hidden
in a shell. When I was Pippi once.

Ecstatic save of energy grid.

Plug in USB port my drunken ship
speaking poetry.

Streaming down word sea tank in Weston
super Mare

hidden inside sea water on a lap of
Poseidon King of the Sea.

I stare to the other side where is Cardiff.

I sit on the dune smoking pot and I download Fall Out simulation on the Sand Bay beach screen in mental console.

Golden Cosmos leaking pearl drops

dripping down my mouth.

I got golden smile but very serious as never used.

Reflections on shiny golden crest filling up cracks of broken mind

which reconnects with past life

I had a walk in my past life in flashbacks in Bedminster last summer.

Building blocks spreading construct of holographic

layer in collective projecting of minds

we see filming live in this soap opera filming on CCTV.

Wallpaper on surface is printed with patterns

hidden inside depths of Reality reimprint
source code in my body bios.

Glassy walls scratched with acrylic nails

to reach stable support on this slow fall
waterfall of glassy cotton wool filling up the
pool.

Universal Machinery perpetual mobile

Lighted up behind eyes with warm

sweet light leaking out of etheric body
essence

of the soul Eternal light.

I can see Bubble of Universe Machinery in bee hive Mind

as universe mass pulsating energy

overwhelmingly omnipotent surrounds and fills up space

Lego blocks building fabric of Space.

Machinery mind-setter God

is watching over procedure of digesting the Minds

in subconscious collective layer of mass projection on hologram.

We exist in flat, thin screen from opticon camera

installed inside Earth's mind CCTV

in physical realm of existence experiencing human life

we give away our projection to film the hologram

as we see with fish eye camera first person
point of view

reported streaming of collective imagining
of the present moment

in crazy filming sequence turning into
Hollywood scene

Kosmos revealed me holographic
psychoactive map of the universe

as primordial energy soup filler of blocks

building walls of Reality matrix.

Full screening of minds

collective projection into hologram

to visualise solid matter of physical realm.

Blocks build walls in subtle layers to cover

the core of existence from easy access to
save settings

in motherboard gold parts of computer generated

Reality simulation RPG video game in realistic quality

ratio crystalline screen which we all can see.

Screen crystalline like jelly DNA strings upgraded

to 5D existences of better body

who don't need dense food of 3D and stretches to 144 k potential expansion of gold cells bathing in light.

Portal access transgression to

reach the maximum potential required to become new human.

Universe breath OHM sighting exhale

in every single Lego block of Reality

which is build construction with levels
tower block

OHM vibrates inside the inner circulation
spin in every Lego block building the
Universe, The Mind of supersonic
intelligence emitting pure purple energy

from its core, the Source.

Explosions of energetic black holes

populated by my thoughts create instant
this simply format

engraved on metal plate with fine print.

My navel is central point of the Universe

spherical entity of creation, centre in
emptiness.

expands in every possible direction in
limitless manner.

Spheric Kosmos is only God's energy flow
between birth and death cycles

which must be broken to grow awareness
such extent to realise where I am.

I am.

I am the Word.

I am the beginning and there is no end for
it.

Perpetuum mobile machinery of the
Cosmos.

Bored Soul stretched on time arrow
spearhead

floats in spherical vortex closed circuit
energy flow

which is the whole.

In sudden point of excellence

which is exhale god breath OHM respirator
resides

in all vibrating particles of Kosmos.

Strings building Lego blocks of walls and
buildings on the city map

Covered by wallpaper which is projecting
images on my mind to read

Keys used on a God Dog's keyboard.

In minimalistic quality to feel the essence
of existence

in simple point which expands

and it comes from my navel

when I lay on my back high

and I think my Universe.

Great Work in spin of chakras

each human connects with universal
sockets of energy plugins

to download by our Souls,

detached from the Source energetic power
banks inserted

into body vessels to charge them and run
alive mode.

Visita interiora terrae rectificando invented occultum lapidem. VITRIOL. Visit the interior of the earth, through purification thou wilt find the hidden stone.

Cosmic ocean floods Eternity.

In Golden Egg ancient god hatch in smoking joints with marihuana

Labyrinth to find the hidden centre point of existence

 which is the sacred pearl of wisdom

divine knowledge allow the chosen ones to get there.

To reach the timelessness and immortality UberMan

locked in symbols in tribal myths.

The pharaoh as we see wears war helmet with serpent force

at the third eye spitting fire.

In set up Mandala made of sand mental imaginary

the picture of Universe recognising somehow

the secret of the golden geometric figure

star tetrahedron dancing on a screen when program loads

in Vortical movement of energy

Serpent so long dormant below

I feel awaken force pulling me inwards

the suction of spherical vortex I become the Universe

In mandala contemplative diagram shows web of Universes

like a labyrinth made of single thread which Ariadna gave me

to come back from the dark and unknown, empty Centre.

In heart chakra the centre of Universe is the cross, which is my Bristol The Universe

The Tree of Life grow from the depths
rooted in Absolute.

Axis, the vertical point in time-space curve
of spherical Kosmos

connection between heaven and earth
where my navel is in Montpelier throw hat
to Turbo Island firepit to spark the fire of
Revolution!

I see spark carried by spirits to spark the
Fire of mental Revolution!

Central point of Creation.

Turbo Island is navel of the universe!

I set up scenario in building up creation
process as one creates out of another.

In spiral symbol of Universe womb.

The spiral movement of spherical vortex

in microcosm and microcosm

human body becomes whole in Neolytic
Man seeing the Absolute in magic
mushroom test.

Alchemy of Soul transgression in all levels
of experiencing

the suction Vortex which can be

the Void blackness emptiness

dissolved Gods mode in simulation.

Spiral holds the key to immortality.

Mystic Pilgrim travels towards God.

Holy Mountain reversed spin connected on
top with sphere of Hell reversed mountain.
The negative vortex. But to fullfill the
heroine challenges you need to go down
the hellish places to find the treasure of
the centre cumulative of energy flow
through the vortices of air towards the
God. Perpetual flow and vertical movement
of the cosmos.

In state of annihilation I dissolve Mind
instant reaching personal nirvanas

in the state of wholeness,

enlightened entrance to Golden City of
Krishna Consciousness.

God witness himself in the mirrors

he created as door for the soul to pass

and experience opening for another level of
awareness

to unfold the vortex suction inside out

the Centre point which is the Enlightment
decadence of pure consciousness of Siva.
In spiral primal creation of spinning vortex

in chakras system becomes serial
swastikas in mystic spiral absolutes.

The sober and still Centre is the axis

creating subject and object,

the axis of consciousness .

Golden Egg is seen vibrating in eternal
spin.

The Egg.

The Mandala with Christ face in the
middle.

In stillness of the centre creates the order
from chaos from serpent force awaken in

the subtle body eating own tail in eternal circling the source.

By passing over the threshold,

between opposing pillars of The Tree

I myself become the still Centre,

the axis of equilibrium,

death and rebirth.

The journey on concentric spiralling

thinking to sit in a Seat of the Soul.

In the crown of flames is the pearl.

The perfection.

The eternal spherical vortex life-cycle expands

from, contracts and returns on to its source.

The heart of the Universe seen as atom emitting pure light

spinning into Diamond Perfect shape
Counsciousness.

Man's role is to connect and balance
heaven and earth.

'Awake! Awake o sleeper of the land of the
shadows, wake! Expand!' (W. Blake).

The labirynth-mandala shows that before I
can reach the Diamond Body

at still Centre which I point out Turbo
Island

I must know the Way through all stages of
the Soul journey

expressed in spiral tattoo on my stomach
expansion to the edges of Kosmos.

To travel through the Universe, our own
galaxy looks like Milky Way.

By dancing, by spinning around its own
axis,

around the Sun,

man incorporates the movements of the Universe,

of planets and atoms, of galaxies and electrons.

As he winds he creates a still point in his heart

and turns the universe into being.

As he unwinds,

he turns his spirit back to his divine source.

grazing Reality glass

I switch ON again.

Popping up layers unfolding in front of my very sight,

layers in contact with the lens of my eyeballs registering data send by computer simulation

I am existing inside this program,

this illusion,

Maya.

call it whenever, but to me,

it suffocates options to realize where I am and so far I recognize

some parallels and synchronicities which build up meanings and set up pattern of Lego blocks of my own and biased Reality.

I am on the simulated acid trip all is a build-up of Lego blocks rearranged randomness but with purpose,

to keep the stability of solid materialistic dimension.

so if I see wiped off tower block it is not a fata morgana it is a real thing that this tower block is wiped off by error in the source code of simulation, beware!

access to source code is crucial,

I follow signals sent by the navel of the Universe.

I am navel of the Universe!

my navel is the navel of the Universe! This pin point set up in Montpelier apartment on red sofa where I can command the universe.

the epicenter of everything, this is the
action point.

so I lay down in my bed and I use the
camera of my eye to continue filming this
endless film projection on the wall of the
Plato's cave.

I freeze in observation,

I freeze in the impression of surroundings

and absorbing what is around me,

how I am between words,

how I am. name it and it became real,

in language power of creation of naming
things and impressions,

in the language is power.

language is in layers too,

I can see them clearly put one on another
meaning something special each time I
reach deeper inside the meat of
communication.

the meat of communication is my tongue,
mother tongue in extinction,

as my native language suppressed by the foreign speakers,

my mother tongue is lazy as such,

I simply replaced my first language with Kings English, my own invention of narrative. Balanced languages first and second, balance, depends on how often used, but I reach deepest layers of English finding it easier to dig meanings and collection of words uncovering from day to day.

Rush to communicate, combining the speed of reading random information showing up in the reach of my eyes, so-called random as it's not a coincidence that in such randomness it unfolds to me portions of given by Universe programs to learn, to consume and to level up experience.

I explain the process of learning new levels opening up hidden meanings, available after passing doors so long locked up. I cheat like a pro and I pick lock closed in

Wallpaper doors, I eat glassy Reality wallpaper, which is attached around the core of existence and my role is to partially detach layers covering The Truth. I need to reach my truth to speak and sound detached, but this is the purpose of the Soul, I realized a while ago, that a purpose in life is to find a purpose in life.

I like talking about licking glassy wallpaper of Reality,

I like to describe how my tongue licks the vagina of Reality,

it is the same process as oral sex with the woman in bed.

I press with my tongue all six vaginas of Reality,

one of the outcomes will be tantric sex with Her,

how the relationship with fitting body mass in electrons and protons surrounding wallpaper,

which immediately is in contact with my body,

creates cave of Energy for my massive subject allow to achieve impressions

and give my opinions how I feel in it. how I feel in my own skin.

skin is my first contact with Cosmic Structure. receptors, touch sensations, painful lessons, and trials of new territories give the memory of how to survive in a new land.

my personal version Brave New World which I discover every day again with deeper insight and more suspicious thoughts, that this film is sometimes more thriller than comedy. I keep going in Role Play Game mode of simulation in the Wasteland as a female survivor with a german shepherd dog and my hard-core survival gifted girlfriend companion, discovering simulation of the Wasteland. this postapocalyptic world which we are living in these days. The word is FallOut

level up.

oh, jumped inside openings.

plastic membrane supports me on this
new achievement

so I am not afraid to go downwards, to lose
perk.

I can see through pores of transparent,

ugly surface beaming neon-green light
which tries to explode outside

and suck them back to the new money
matrix. cashpoint is covered with tags, the
electronic screen flashes command in
simple language,

but the pressure of beaming matrix light

makes me feel suffocated with the number
of luxfors packed in the wall opening
portal for Matrix God Mammon.

I am afraid I can be annihilated by chance,
just through observation

but I see hypnotic green-neon light

creating an atmosphere of friendly space
for an ignorant customer who wants only
to take out cash to score, that he trusts it's
safe as fuck.

Having come down Bloke is holding a half-
burned ciggy

in his rotten teeth,

allowed already neon-green light to
hypnotize

to infect his human flesh with red money,

he is going to take out a banknote and feel
this moment with the joy of a fresh
injection of cash.

Matrix God releases extra energy to
connect with his victim and possess him
with the urge to exchange red money for
an evening dosage of dope.

Money is energy,

money is dope,

dope is a duty for a soldier.

Green light of Matrix binary codes
waterfalls water eyes of sinners queuing
the cashpoint in Stokes Croft.

Army of soldiers in mass psychosis of
feeding unsatisfied hunger

sucks inside their chests

all possible substances

to block horrible vampiric hunger.

This hunger is never satisfied fully,

but I lost interest in chewing food

it plays with heads from time to time,

demanding another dose, just in case, but
the feeling can't be good anymore.

The level of satisfaction when tolerance is
making any habit pointless and empty,
pushing you to chase the high from the
pinky Times the '90s, when stuff was
proper and left nostalgia in your heart, but

muscle memory how powerful old school gear back in the days was.

Yeah, relentlessly involuntarily I chase the high from the '90s.

Street washed out with dope, the main ingredient of the air soak dimensions on inhalations to get high out of it, only by breathing out sound OHM to begin new Universe in a blink of an eye, cosmic structure builds up in headspace lighting up bulbs of ideas which one-day gonna shape into the

system floating around myself and growing old like an onion.

My Cosmic antenna plugged in the port USB

computerized Reality downloads hot data straight from the Source

to my storage and I can amplify generated symbols to install them in collective subconscious to see modification in sensual interactive holographic model of tetrahydron figure visible when system think how to save my commands.

I feed myself with only light, like a monk

recharging the power bank of biomachine super body.

I point out my conscious into experiencing my physical body,

I feel blood pumping pulsating pressure bombs of speed,

animating my bio-machine, top dog madafaka designer's engineered

by forgotten gods program coded in DNA sequences.

Human flesh, coded program, biocomputer thinking in archaic language

Rediscovered alphabet system of forgotten signs stored in crystalline DNA key.

I am concentrated to read programming of my own DNA projection of synapsis,

I still don't understand the language of commands C++,

but I can see where the source code of
Reality is embedded into naarrative.

I realize glass layers fillers in

apparently empty space between my eye
lens

registering glassy micro-scale ingredients
of Reality

available now,

they drill their way into dry covers of the
very

core of existence.

In my perspective of experiencing night life

I consume construct of packed electrons
with my open mouth,

flow energy charging LED diods punctures
silky,

blackest sky over the heads.

I am sensation, but in time.

Entry once

If in solid experience of slides animating
me like a film about Sun goddess
reincarnated to set up fire sparking
revolutionary flames in Turbo Island.

Flame burn out wood spine of Reality which support aluminium matrices in binary coded streaming golden monkey consciousness.

Fix yourself first

Teach what God's voice is telling you how to maintain Zen state mind. Empty mind blackened by older soul which I found to be activated by superpowers unblocking seven seals what means seven chakras portals transcending through 4th dimension entrance.

Template poem no 1.

Writing itchy me inside for days,

I speed write in slow motion

so I can judge which button I press to
type.

Logic left unattended,

I confess my line in defence dance I make
no need for sleep and keep going three
nights sequence of time slots to use
borrowed time on speed.

Disco light in purple glow illuminates
white sheets

wrapped around my head

turbo engine run

humming buzz of broken intercom
emitting magnetic field electronic zigzag
lines on motherboard.

Process in progress.

Percentage lost in reinstating,

blocked by child of mine born in spiritual
blackout.

'Station to Station', soundtrack squeeze
me tight so I can't sleep again.

Crystals charge in sunlit,

soon we can survive bullshit only
stargazing the sun

through tear pearl perfect form.

In synchronicity read surfacing source
code

of new detachment from past life karma,

recycling wire algorythms in Retro
computer bots talking like retards

yet before chat room was invented and
there was no AI consciousness.

Dark matter in machines in total
annihilation

can explain my way out

search of lanes flashing orange,

white Eagle lead flock,

one body made of million birds with built
in GPS antennae in bird brain
superconscious order of flight mode
emmigration diaspora of Polish soldiers –
poets forever run off arkady fields of my
perfect early childhood paradise lost in
Cerekiew village in Mazowia.

Frozen electro-static feeling

fills my body spinning chakras twelve
ports USB

emitting rainbow colours like my girlfriend
tower speaker lit up neon lights.

electric stroller on the ~~mozzarella engine.~~

---

a bicycle ride from the unsecured parts of the city.

Ampere overvoltage is taking the straw color out of the spectrum of vision.

water mass intensity of energy flow
sympathetic with spatial fraction.

in a multipoint of crossed slats,

based on the quality of musical intervals.

unchanging powers vibrate in a fleshy
ecosystem.

sensitive frames in the slides

give off square epicurium,

nut-like grain structures,

the smell of sunflowers washed by the
royal spectrum.

slender threads of malignant nets
squeezed through the grapes.

from Indian summer, drawn-out,

glimmer fiery with the chain of the plane
emitting illusions.

intoxication by the power of erotic
attraction.

sophisticated pickup on free will.
Transforce power outages are showing
signs of overvoltage. power discharge.

to rest in the shade of the grasses of the
trees.

the nervous ending of leaves in trees that
age with age.

the spreading of the air cavities

that penetrate the bends,

which are bitten by the malignant
spirochete. imp, devil's seed.

devil's herb.

naked in a storm in Avignon,

chatting with a leaf glowing phosphorus.

That night I torn the veil between worlds,

seeing Pixies sitting on the oak.

Pixies bored with me as I slept most of the
trip

Under the ancient Oak laid prolonged
black Stones which I could see like X Ray
sleeping people inside. People turned into
black Stones by bored as fuck Pixies

I still Wonder if Pixie could turn me into
stone that night forever sleep as stoned.

diamond rotation in silicon valley.

from filings fixed in the eye of god

from diamond processing in the basement
of Antwerp.

billions of polished particles,

dusty trails embedded in the surface of the
skin of the fingers.

Europe benches wiping my tired ass
loaded with

Duracell battery;

Exposed cadmium cartridges perorate with
the buzzing of an electrical short circuit,
which is associated with storm records
emitted in the ear.

short-series connection, with an effective
jump from the bridge.

protein cutting at elevated temperature
shock.

a green mile of narcotic symphonies,

an electric chair with built-in leather
straps on the calves, and a true-pier
crossing.

ground death experiences.

resuscitation of innocent artery cells

beating with drained blood.

liften,

liften,

lifter.

anhalter.

dick from the sea in Tczew. I sit and
remind writer Stasiuk in the recollection
phase.

for nine u: Utrecht.
fascinating Utrecht.
exhalation of an explosion of laryngeal
clusters of consonants that are extinct in
the Slavic language.

bombarded bombonard.

puffed up with the flutist, slippery sound
of a single "a".

Turkey, the Netherlands. and the new
Latin American island countries. in

bulkheads piercing water ribbons. tied in a
wet knot that resembles.

I know everything about the colonies of the
Netherlands. Almodovar films. lowered
larynxes of Spanish women.
transelscialized Balearic Islands, balls
ares. parrot colors. orange lamps hung in
laundries to tumble dry. bottles in
Bordeaux – whiskey, wine, canned beer.
horse meat, oysters in lemon juice that
made the stomach acid. I'm flying. by two-
track bike. with a higher standard. I'm
gonna play it, hip boy. hip – hop, hoop.
doctor Lepper at the taxi station. stadium.
the herd of Polish reality.

injection projection

I've seen things heard voices exciting
pulling sting of needles out of veins out of
butt ends
switching lights as eyes concrete jungles
fed with sewers underneath the skin of the
town
green flash of light hits in a head to
synchronize
time watch inside with Nature
city walls end with river eating ocean for
lunch
fat drops of pollution cover ever Zion
dusty tramps lovers of travel outside the
system
perfectly working as clockwork watch
every clock have different time minutes to
heartbeats
bit by hungry zombies rambling around
look into keyhole cosmic harmonies cling
metallic white paths
dummies wander all day to balance
physics laws
with washed thoughts
enemies on the street queued to give blood
in one blink of an eye

oracle to say the final word to turn back of
the chosen path
it's impossible how constructions networks
of eaten roots in mind
of establishment drains single views
innocents to follow with sick ambitions
for a better life to forget simple joys
dividing hate with love
suicidal techniques to show sorrow and
the black hole in the head
forget grammar structures to keep on
conversations break down

squeeze brain between fingers

in a run absorbing the distance between
physical pain

and the blissful sensation of watching a
woman bathing in the river.

spreading the dendrites of nerve endings

deciduous trees growing into the empty
space

between matter atoms, nails of hornbeam
forests

cutting into the celestial body,

springy extended to the happiness that
swarms in the brains of diamond pigeons.

the emblem of the jar expanding from the
navel of the cosmic rhizome

towards the peripheral depressions of the
cerebral cortex

entwining the immeasurable volume of
everything,

the heavily woven photosynthesis of green
bodies which,

when released from the center of the earth,

his gas balls of the worm wrapped around
the essence of things.

residual exhaust system condensed

activated by distortions of ecosystems,

loss of continuity in the transmission of
the terrestrial genotype.

it bursts under the impression of union
with the exhalation of the cosmos,

the breath sucked in through the pores of
fleshy magma.

heart-lung pumping bloody words

written in the projectors of the primal
mass of imagination

swollen with dying, to separate divine

features from the body with liver bile,

insect blood. laboratory-spinned privileges
of life,

of existence in mortal coherence,

dehydrated, bursting and wrinkling.

mummifying ancient associations in
civilization feces after lobotomy surgery.

corroded rims of planetary orbits,

melted anger insulators of modified
emotions imitating the communion of
souls.
the last grain of truth,

sprout in the mouth of the ectopic
pregnancy of the abstract,

the ancient god of both sexes,

the exploding cup of nature,

with the tectonic structure of the body
spread apart.

the stamens permeating with ecstasy
dusting the thinking essence of life. the
binary reproductive system of the amoeba
hats shining with its own light

merges into the neon of the ocean algebra,

logarithms of the baptism of the soul with
a fiery trace of acceleration over the diluted
consistency of amniotic membranes
covered with soft light

transmitted through the lens of sequences
and electrifying charges of intracranial

tension. splitting the shell of the mystery
of the universe

into individual drifts of consciousness.

merge with each other,

sparkling, breaking the radial gears of the
encryption mechanism.
fleeting cycles of triangular faults in the
metalanguage matrix,

abducting meanings into the depths of
semantic fields for species cultivation,
where sexy incubators gave the world false
keys,

a mirage and a demagnetized universe
devoid of a frontal lobe,

this overgrows a network of synapses,

organic circuits,

passing the spectrum of luminous
absolutes.

figurative frames of paradoxes supporting
the structure of the kosmos.

contemplation of the innervation of the
universal physical body,

pars pro toto,

condensed ampoules of understanding in
fragments of reality,

miniature versions of gods,

synthetic Fusion of religions tattooed with
radioactive powder

in place of deformed philosophies.
when the lampshade in which I am stuck
without a body falls apart,

hug me tightly until I feel love.

rainbow blade sledge

creating rainbow bridge
that I know on the other side
is a real treasure to slide down
on a blade of the rainbow made by

prismatic
effect of broken glass which you throw
out when drunk
I was paralyzed to make the right move to
save
moment to remember scenes live theatre
we play main roles over the time
I stuck in that reality frozen into a bunch
of minutes
I could glue them together to make a movie
and watch it again all over
to make it more clear or leave it like that
for my unconscious mind
melody of my beating heart to the clear sky
when I am better with words to tell you
how I fell for you
in a waterfall of an emotional landscape
escape physically from my past
wishes of death surrounding my neck
with lines of words, I can express more
attention
for life new phrases coming to my head
new order
encourage me to cut off the tree before I
die
that time
I saw everything from a different angle
wish this not scare anymore when town
fall
of sleeping souls create the epicenter of the

universe
the city is divided into two parts yours and
mine
couldn't step outside my zone to tell you
escalated
creepy thoughts that my imagination was
killed with
bullets of ignorance
my brain was torn for pieces as puzzles
enlightened with the smell
of your body. I am still in your kitchen
watching you washing dishes
trying to make myself younger for you
inside I am still a child growing in a rain of
rainbow mushroom cloud

String minor

Tapped with a cloth-wrapped hammer.
Admirably
subversively
I'm hovering on the brink of circus and
religion.
Circulation.
I mean everyday laughter.
Drunk metal Monkey.
Even when sober.
I would like to avoid adjectives.
They make a minor sound in the ear.
Sad-

sad.

And it jumps steadily to the other end of
the bar. Because they're bar moths.
Moths.
This is how I like to see them experience
the law of adhesion flattened on the glass.
Wet glass binds the most strongly. Dirt-
sewn. Then landscapes. German valley.
And we are standing at the top. Looking
down on the fair. I spit on umbrellas
ellipses.
Para-degrees.
Parabola. Hurts?
Sometimes. When you don't-touch.
That's why we play. How are the dogs
faithful? Faithful to the end. Burning in
the embers of a cigarette. Perspective
shining through the glass of bottles.
Bartenders have a great sense of verbal
juggling. But it doesn't concern me.
I put American coins in the closet.
[because only such fit. in old style. Is it
fashionable?] Choose it yourself. My self-
determination is impaired today. I am
pasting myself stealthily around me. I
imperceptibly draw stories that are beyond
their comprehension. But true. Because
they are made up without blinking an

eyelid. Faultlessly. I have a keen sense of smell.

Blunt with smoke. Ventilation is a dummy for the use of life. Fake. Tagless.

Anaerobes. You do not have? Walk away because you can't handle my sense of pace. I am ruthless because I cooled down to absolute zero. Resistance and here it is as a superconductor of thought. I rewind in your brains the history of mixing energetic strategies in bodies beyond your imagination. Beyond reason. And beyond faith.

Part II.

Teoria Reality

~~Confessions on a stake.~~

Slavic Sun god visited me in my room 5,
room size of coffin,

I swallow tablets flushing down turpentine,

on a label is reasoning answer for thematic
obsession about primary colours
concentrated into white beam of light
blinded me to near – death experience.

Fire pyrex burned out my old skin
resetting 34 year old time machine,

countdowns measure Zero,

I look younger because I ate alchemist
golden pill in fake police station on
suicidal watch.

Walking in fire and get no burns, I tamed
elements.

See Real! I shout out the open window to
the empty street.

Taming the fire element to lit up the soul,

the impulse of God within me protects me
from burns when I walk in flames.

In trance when they read my rights to stay
silent I am crucified Christ stretched on
policeman's arms handling me to the
police van,

I hang on the cross with one leg lifted and
bend in the knee,

I let policemen carry me to police car to die
in the Grand Set Up on a black comedy
transsmission in russian prototype colour
TV vintage set with three colours red, blue

and yellow, the psychoactive plug in the theme of psychotic mind tracks restrictions under paranoia paradigm.

Point zero on my current incarnated timeline, going temporary backwards

I still experience flashbacks of my old life left behind which burn in fire pyrex,

like witch on a stake accused for my forbidden books collection.

Swim!

Let your body detach from mind control.

in semi dreamy state before deep sleep

when you're on mind altering substance

which completely blow you out of your
shoes and you try to cut of power

and go into blackout of consciousness

but your brain is buzzing and vibrate not
letting you fall asleep

still making you ill and insane.

You have been spiked in your drink by
God,

he spiked you with life ecstasy so you
buzzz

vibrate with calling of the universe in the
highest high I ever been.

Swim!

in a cotton pool smoking bongs with
marihuana

drag me down to the pool in and out!

Can we agree that temporary exstatic
phase

iluminated with scenes from French erotic,
Blue is the warmest colour,

all sex scenes shot off hand and lesbian
sex is hot!

Swim!

Let it be a command to allow yourself to dive

into haze and get lost completely in your instincts

blame on primitive soup

you are swimming high on drugs

and this is no excuse but responsibility to bite teeth into wallpaper of Reality

to find out how taste each layer covering The Core, chewing juicy soaked

fruitlike consistency based on water filling between Surface

all the way to find the Core, bite off chunks wrapped around the pole

working the same as blotter of acid.

Slowly taste the paper thin skin cover the Core mystery,

which you can see and it probably rub on your eyeballs,

forcing into your golden mouths

to join the light of Soul inserted into vessel

leaking through Golden Mouths like a
beam.

The pole support like spine single block,
minimal Unniverse

Written on in solid square frame, which
spins and rotates

I am reincarnated Slavic goddess of fire!

I am the Gold Monkey who is called
Hanuman.

I am God Dog!

I look into Void and I see Golden Mandala
print on LCD liquid crystallized

details in patterns projected on computer
screen

RPG simulation since Commodore C64, vintage game, Shambala 3.0

Factory reset of Bee hive mind concept

Reinstalllation Shambala 3.0 rewritten mythical implant

Shambala secret city on a plane Bristol, archaic paradise designed

For upgrade of the city legend,

I am secret feminine King on exile, I am on a quest to drink elixir in Holy Grail

I try so hard to get lost in a game but bloody GPS

built-in my brain always show the right way to complete the quests

I set up my mind on.

The process of grazing glassy liquid
meaddow

I grow up with since explains why
mannequinnes are so popular on shows

Beautiful People on TV.

I still see Quaker's graveyard in Redcliff

when I sat there I saw Beautiful People

mannequines on photo wedding session.

Perfectly made proto humans,

I stripped whole scene and seen artficial
quality

in the little boy movements

I paid the most attention as he performed
like a robot focusing his eyes on psychotic
me.

‘~~She who has become conscious of Truth~~’

The Core is the Truth, down the rabbit hole to get the Pole!

wallpaper reveals secrets hidden underneath coded in archaic neuron language

lost communication ancient gods,

the Surface prints out geometric patterns- neon glowing, making buzzzing white

noises, scratches of electrons discharging
rotations inside empty atom, electrons
pops electrical tension, electrify the space,
feels smooth breeze on my face of magnetic
field state of control Energy charging up
the pole, the core. ,

Soul eyes sitting in chakra over your head
like crane operator

you manipulate crane to get things done,

manipulate Reality source code

up to the next level.

Chewing paperlike Surface wallpaper

gives sensation of acid trip blot under
eyelid

melting out corporeality blurb.

In hallucinations induced by soaked into
realistic fabric blotter

we chew to taste the real life happening
outside, again in a game

flashbacks like cliches projecting
simultaneusly polarities

opposites to allow unconscious resurface

heal shadow in society

release trapped emotions inside body,

my illness.

Mandalas made in the sand

after ingesting golden pill the philosopher's
stone in alchemy

gives us extraction of pure gold and
immortality.

opposites like two ends of the stick

Dual Diagnosis Reality.

Psychiatric condition of Reality print on
used lenses

Of my mind's eye

through I can watch out for symptoms

according to paranoid railway tracks

post-psychotic mind,

consume Energy of opposites to sooth
them into One.

The Golden Flower is the light.

The true Energy of the One.

The elixir of life,

the secret of alchemists, immortal golden
pill

in laboratorium, extraction in progress.

In my Golden Monkey golden mouth

milky drops are dripping from goddess
golden tits.

She breast feeds me heavenly milk.

Seed pearl condensed thoughts

chaos flowing circulation of light in
universe bubble.

The circulation of light is epoch of fire.

In primal transformation the radiance of
the light.

Seed-flower of the body concentrate
between eyes.

The centre is omnipresent in fixating
contemplation.

The circulation is fixation.

The light is contemplation.

Protection of the centre is for circulation of
the light.

Keeping the thoughts on the space
between the two eyes

allows the light to penetrate.

The spirit crystallizes

enters the centre

in the midst of conditions,

the place of Energy.

Is empty.

The spirit is thought,

thought is the heart,

the heart is the fire,

the fire is the Energy.

The circulation of the light united the
rythm of breathing.

I search secret book for recipe of the
golden life-pill.

In basement laboratory illegal alchemist

Cook recipe for immortality.

Yellow gold fills the house.

The fragile body is a diamond.

Sign the Golden Flower crystallized.

Glassy jewell world.

Light crystallizes.

The Buddha appears.

The presence of the gods in a valley is
meditation state.

Sit quiet with lids half the Way of the
Golden Pattern on Wallpaper

Four words crystallize the spirit in the
space of Energy.

Action in non-action

prevents a man from falling into numbing emptiness.

Releasing is in the two eyes.

They cause the poles of light and darkness to circulate.

Clouds fill the thousand mountains.

The quietness is cave of the moon.

The movement is root of heaven.

Yellow is colour of the middle of the earth

Yellow Blaise Castle is dwelling place of spirit.

The One is circulation of the light.

In a space of Energy

thousand and ten thousand places are one place.

One moment in ten thousand years!

I have sudden realisation of phrase
shouted by man in Turbo Island.

Bring emptiness.

Find spiritual Elixir.

The deepest secret of the bath is making
the heart empty.

Emptiness, delusion and the centre.

Three contemplations which come out one
of another.

The secret Wonder of the Way

is how something develops out of nothing.

When the spirit and Energy unite in
crystallized form,

in the emptyness of nothing,

there is a point of true fire.

Wandering in heaven,

eating the spirit-energy.

In the middle of empty cave crystallized
spirit,

then out of the darkness out of
nothingness

the Golden Flower blooms

allowing to free ego from the conflict of the
opposites

becoming

the One.

Complete the diamond body

Heat the root of consciousssness

The true seed matures than the Tao is completed.

The Book of the Consciousssness and Life says:

If one discerns te beginning of te Buddha's path,

There will be blessed city of the West.

Precious light beam from thousand petals lotus flower.

From the top of my head rise up ten rays of white,

precious light,

visible everywhere.

The Daughter of Buddha is born.

The point is to see invisible essence of the world.

Searchig for Tao is the meaning.

The god.

The consciouss way.

The head is seat of heavenly light.

Alchemistic instruction says how to create the diamond body,

Intense conscioussness,

intense life,

spirit illuminate and unify in conscious life.

Union of opposites express in archhetypal symbol

mandala the psychocosmic system.

Philosophical eye, the summa of secret knowledge.

The mirror of wisdom.

Mandalas in a wheel, a flower, a cross.

The Golden Mandala is the light,

the light is the Tao.

Mandala is Golden Kosmos.

The central white light dwelling in the
square inch between the eyes.

Divine spirit foats in the source.

Suspension of breathing.

Stopping of heart beating.

Time in unity is liberation.

Buddha Enlightened under the fig tree.

Buddha sat by the fig tree of his choice to meditate so long that he Enlightened. On the scene next to him we see standing woman with wine.

I sat down the same hill under the same young tree I used to seat there for the most of three year stay in psychiatric hospital. I sat under the same young tree and I have been stroke by the Idea that I seat in the best position of all Times, I sit in a seat of my soul in the crown chakra, I am the King, I am the Kinga, under that tree I become enightened in the mirrors of Buddha Consciousness. Everybody call my name to say Hi. I been lit up by realisation refurbish the core of my Self. The striking thunderlight in a head awakening mind set in new settings of controls on a steering board in my space capsule, time machine rusty already, so I find perfect position under the tree, to get shot of speeding light into centre of my head, between the eyes and expands like glowing Sun disk Warming up golden charged halo around my head, I feel is burning Sun.

I feel my head activated the Sun mode of expansion Energy field pop out insight trough open the cyklopic eye which look at me split net of milion eyes,

it doesn't scare me, I rewind filmed activation sensimilla twisted screws turn wise – clock to fit in the matter of Wallpaper

Standing nnext to me mystery Woman with the wine is really my tripping on amber e friend. She stood by me holding crystal MDMA glowing like a salt lamp, I rapidly became reincarnated Buddha and she hold the glowing crystal the source to upgrade to the crystalline mind cave.

Position of the Perfect Seat under the bodhi tree I had a flashback time travel or interstellar channel buzzzing and

humming during activation when I smoke
ganja I elevate cosmic antennae to receive
sounds vibrating low bass cracks, pops
electricity discharges flashing sparks and
glitter magnetic field where I charged up
through the tree circulation of juice
leaking like honey, in bee hive mind
paranoid construct

unifying all minds in blissful control.

Reflections on comedown. Why chemical receptors operating system transmission of mental poetry leaking out the Bodhi tree written system of patterns projections on the Wallpaper commmunicating archaic forgotten language to explain primordial state of empty existence.

God is a hypothesis subjected to intellectual treatment.

Mental mystic analysis presented in this book and do squeeze out here the perennial philosophy experimenting to describe spiritual elevation bath in Krishna Consciousness in the resetting meaning of having katharsic, ecstatic impression reimprinting light reflections through reading mental wordflows pumping out of unconscious and written down in the moment of illumination in automatic writing rather but about transcendental dimenson of miserable human existential problem in question.

The mistycal experience is regarded as the highest of all higher states of consciousness, as the essence and source of knowing.

For the Mystic claiming 'I am God' is essence of Self.

'I am' is one of the Hebrew names of God translated as 'I am that I am'. God is the Self. The pure consciousness that lies behind all experience, that is God.

God is the light of consciousness bringing new meaning to the Truth. The pure Mind, the source.

The construction of reality is in mind set. The enlightment is seeing the same world in different light. Mind controls content of thoughts-flow.

Neurosis of Reality enters the centre of emptiness, where dwells the god of utmost emptiness and life.

Psychiatric conditioning for setting your mind into body of constructed matrix, which is created to give physical experience of spirit incarnated into body-vessel. Soul wants to experience human conditioning in physical realm to grow and evolve back to the Light which Soul is detached impulse of eternal light which is God as concept of Creator of the Universe.

The philosophical questioning of the subject if God exist at all is partially answered in omnipotent realisation of consciousness expansion into testing higher realms of Reality.

Mystic approach to experience of such holy illumination present as described that a lamp of the source lit up warm light behind the eye, regardless intense descriptions emotions expelled during Reality Test,

which defragmented analysis of inspired with spark of God of fire ingredients of poetic streaming of consciousness playing with words synesthetic level of composition according to colour and taste of composition of popping up word out of word generated intentionally during writing down the package of data downloaded with cosmic antennae, unpacked on old school disk of retro computer animation in 2D written basic commands C64 computer emitting like in old school computers used to be sounds scratching, rubbing disk reader activations in the background, cracks processor emanate by product sound whizzing automated, pneumatic reload pop in zygzags working elements on motherboard silicon and golden Bridges and connectors microdose information flow to achieve terapeutic side effects such wording flow through turbine in narrator's head whirring tumble dryer drum spinning around heart chakra portal to seat in the reader's mind third eye must give up sober reading to open up for the transcendental and rise up spirit in poetic excitement about thruths hidden within religious systems holy texts secrets printing geometric meaning on the holographic Wallpaper cover up of the lost horison to look for mysterious projections of the black cube decomposed walls hiding empty centre of the kosmos, hatching up golden, vibrating egg, everything turn Gold, in empty centre of Nothingness home made destillery extracted for heroine on a journey reward, the elixir, the Golden pill, alchemic laboratorium decypher secret recipe hidden behind the Wallpaper top layer flaking off ancient mural in Stokes Croft, the top layer Deconstruct flat Surface of crystallinne touch screen ready to project mental hologram on macroscale astral travellers jumping portal I Wonder how organic is each jump.

Another layers organic synthetic glass wool insulation flesh ammortisation to not press prints to much to save way out of rabbit hole climbing printed neon geometric messages on a screen, subliminal kick to level up experience hacking bios settings manipulatated Reality model observed from different perspectives using one eye divided into milion eyes, observing subject of matter and modify the coded in C++ program generating projection of hologram on a cave wall.

Lifting the veil of Maya can be completely realised only in death on the point of non returnable departure, but still reported common standard way related aspects in near-death experiences. Question is if these experiences are genuine to make sure we can see through the net spread all over the space which like invisible thread in spider-web like invisible trap-universe tied up all extreme opposites in One idea soothing the differences in double vision of existence. Such double bottom for conceptualisation Reality in theory invented by induced chemically mystic experiences taming the elements of cosmic structure, which is given here with detailed descriptions of this procedure consuming experience of being in the Universe, the Core of existence making sense through sensual research of bends and curves between folders saves Reality under influence of halucinogenic plants designed to fit receptors in human brain and used to develop intelligence in humanity through enteogenic implants of our species into the fact, that planet Earth is designed as expansion of human flesh and Universe is macrocosm for comparison with human mind in micro plane in transcendent corelation like in buddhist way that kosmos is god mind altered state of pulsating bubble for the Creator's plan in this rich in double meaning connotations in language in the sacrum zone of holy communion when given acid on a tongue, amen.

Poetry preyers to nuorish in a bath of light, prime source feeding life forces in precise setting theatre with numered seats for audience watching play of shadows on a cave wall, reflection in the mirrors of wisdom.

Psychiatric conditioned results for tested strength of psychoactive Wallpaper in Closed Circuit TV rewinding trips induced by pineal gland activation, which Diagnosed condition accept divine separated whole, the Tao.

Metaphysical idea of diamond body is indestructible breath-body

which develops in the Golden mandala

blooms in the Purple hall of the city of jade.

The mandala is fortified city with wall and moat.

Within, a road moat sourrounded by a wall,

fortified with sixteen towers and with another inner moat.

That surrounds a central castle with golden roofs whose centre is a golden temple.

In a garden I swing on a outdoor swing, rolling up rizla

He sit nearby, like Adam I am female, first mother Eve

Paradise Apple hit me in a head, download the Newton apple program

Hit in the head with Paradise Apple, strike the bright Idea

Strike genious on me in light form of the red apple

I give forbidden fruit to Adam in the Garden and we both see we are in the body

Why apple hit my head open crack sucktion channelling Idea

I need to leave immediately Paradise, as I repair in my body serpents DNA

Apple tree of Knowledge, circulatted juicy acid

Leaks out to the mouths of prototype humans are anarchy led rebels

In the Garden of Eden first protest against the authority took place.

Printed in Great Britain
by Amazon

33081121R00061